Newcomen Primary School.,
Trent Road,
Redcar,
Cleveland.   TS10 1ND

# ANCIENT
# EGYPT

# STRUAN REID

Belitha Press

## Acknowledgements

### Photographic Credits

page 2: Louvre, Paris, Egyptian wooden statue, 2100 BC
page 3: Hutchinson Library, Bernard Regent, Giza pyramids and camels
page 4: Mansell Collection, etching by David Roberts of the interior of the temple of Abu Simbel, 1836
page 6: Robert Harding, death mask of Tutankahmun
page 8: British Museum, the cat goddess Bastet
page 10: Cairo Museum, the mummified head of Pharaoh Rameses II
page 12: British Museum, Shabti tomb dolls
page 14: Wellcome Foundation, statue of Imhotep
page 16: British Museum, statue of the scribe Pes-shu-per
page 18: British Museum, two model boats
page 20: British Museum, wall painting of fishing scene
page 22: British Museum, magic stick
page 24: British Museum, gold bracelets
page 26: Ronald Sheridan, chair owned by a pharaoh's daughter
page 28: British Museum, paddle doll

Editor: **Jill A. Laidlaw**
Specialist consultant: **George Hart**, British Museum
Designed by: **John Calvert**
Picture research: **Ann Usborne**
Illustrated by: **Peter Massey**
With thanks to **James Puttnam** of the British Museum

First published in the UK in 1993 by
 Belitha Press Limited,
London House, Great Eastern Wharf,
Parkgate Road, London SW11 4NQ
Reprinted 1993, 1997
Illustrations/photographs copyright © in this format by Belitha Press Limited 1993
Text copyright © Struan Reid 1993
Illustrations copyright © Peter Massey 1993
ISBN 1 85561 158 9
Typeset by Chambers Wallace, London

British Library Cataloguing in Publication Data CIP data for this book is available from the British Library

Printed in Hong Kong

# CONTENTS

*Words found in **bold** are explained in the glossary on pages 30 and 31*

## Finding Egypt

Let's go far away to Egypt and travel back in time to this hot, dry country in North Africa. On the southern shores of the Mediterranean Sea the civilisation of Ancient Egypt began nearly 7,000 years ago. The greatest kings of Egypt were the Pharaohs. They began ruling Egypt 5,000 years ago and their rule lasted 3,000 years.

Lush, green fields hugged the banks of the River Nile and it is here that most of the Ancient Egyptians lived. They built huge stone temples, tombs and rich works of art, many of which have survived and can be seen in museums all over the world.

*This globe shows where Egypt is in the world (above).*

*This map shows an area of Ancient Egypt. Most people lived beside the River Nile where the land was green and fertile (right).*

*This is an etching of the inside of the ruined temple of Abu Simbel (left). You can see how massive Egyptian temples are by how small the people look. It was drawn in 1836 by David Roberts, a Scotsman who painted and drew many of the sights of Egypt.*

## Your Own Museum

You can see some of the things the Egyptians made in this book. It is your own personal museum. It introduces you to the Ancient Egyptians themselves. By asking questions about some of the objects they have left us we can build up an exciting picture of life in Ancient Egypt. Come and look at the sort of houses people lived in, the clothes they wore and how they travelled. Come and read about their belief in life after death, their mummies, pyramids and magic wands.

5

## Q: What is this object?

A: This is the gold mask of the Pharaoh Tutankhamun. He ruled from 1333-1323 BC. The mask was put on his face when he was buried. His tomb was discovered in 1922.

## Q: Who was the Pharaoh?

A: Many kings of Egypt were called Pharaoh. This word means 'Great House' in Egyptian. The Ancient Egyptians called the king 'Ruler of Upper and Lower Egypt'. The people of Egypt believed that the Pharaoh was a god. They thought that when he sat on his throne and gave his orders, all the other gods of Egypt spoke through him.

## Q: Was the Pharaoh married?

A: The Pharaoh could have many wives, but only one was called Great Royal Wife. Because he was a god, no ordinary person could marry him and become his queen. He often married a member of his own family.

*The king and queen are wearing their official crowns. The king holds the crook standing for kingship. In his other hand is the flail standing for the fertility of the land of Egypt.*

7

8

**Q: What have cats got to do with religion?**
A: This cat is a goddess. Her name is Bastet. She is shown as a cat or as a human with a cat's or lion's head.

**Q: Where was Bastet worshipped?**
A: The Egyptians built temples for their gods and goddesses to live in. Only the priests, priestesses and the Pharaoh and queen could worship the gods in their temples.

**Q: Did the Egyptians worship only Bastet?**
A: The Egyptians worshipped many gods and goddesses. They were usually shown as humans with an animal head.

**Q: Was Bastet the most important god?**
A: The Sun was the most important god. The Egyptians had many versions of the Sun god, but Re was the most common. They believed that Re created the world. Re is usually shown as a hawk with the Sun above his head.

*The ceremony of feeding Bastet in her temple.*

9

**Q: Is this the head of an Ancient Egyptian?**

A: This is the Egyptian Pharaoh Rameses II. He died 3,000 years ago. His body was discovered in 1881. He still has his teeth, hair and skin.

**Q: How did his body survive so long?**

A: The Egyptians believed that when a person died they passed on to another life in the next world. Because of this it was very important to keep the dead person's body complete when it was buried. Otherwise their spirit, or Ka, would be unable to return to its body in the next life. The body was **preserved** so that the spirit had a home. This is called mummification. Rameses II's body has been so well preserved that we can tell he was about ninety when he died.

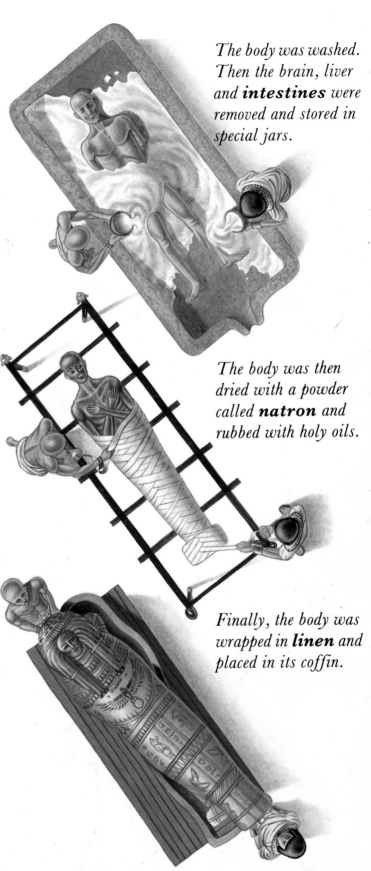

*The body was washed. Then the brain, liver and **intestines** were removed and stored in special jars.*

*The body was then dried with a powder called **natron** and rubbed with holy oils.*

*Finally, the body was wrapped in **linen** and placed in its coffin.*

## Q: What is in this box?

A: This wooden box contains wooden dolls called shabti figures. They were made 4,000 years ago and put in a tomb.

## Q: Why were they put in tombs?

A: Shabti figures were supposed to do all the hard work on behalf of the dead person in their next life (see page 11).

## Q: What were Egyptian tombs like?

A: Most people in Ancient Egypt were buried in simple graves in the ground. But if you were very rich you could afford to have a very **elaborate** tomb. Some of the Pharaohs were buried deep inside huge tombs called pyramids.

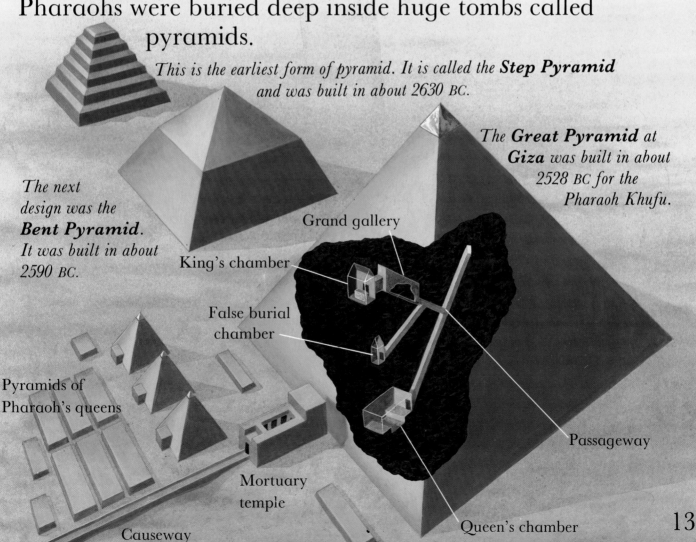

*This is the earliest form of pyramid. It is called the **Step Pyramid** and was built in about 2630 BC.*

*The **Great Pyramid** at **Giza** was built in about 2528 BC for the Pharaoh Khufu.*

*The next design was the **Bent Pyramid**. It was built in about 2590 BC.*

Grand gallery

King's chamber

False burial chamber

Pyramids of Pharaoh's queens

Passageway

Mortuary temple

Causeway

Queen's chamber

13

14

## Q: Who is this a statue of?

A: This is Imhotep. He lived about 4,600 years ago. Imhotep was Vizier or the head of the government of the Pharaoh **Djoser**. He also designed the Step Pyramid for Djoser and was a skilled doctor.

*The Vizier is kneeling before the Pharaoh. He is reading out all the important news for the day.*

## Q: What did a Vizier do?

A: A Vizier was the Pharaoh's chief **minister** and was one of the most powerful people in the land. Every day he reported to the Pharaoh and told him what was going on in the country.

## Q: How was Egypt ruled?

A: The Pharaoh ruled his country with the help of his government officials. The government was divided into three main **departments**. One department looked after the money, another looked after relations with other countries, and the third controlled all the building projects.

16

## Q: Who is this?
A: This is a stone statue of a scribe called Pes-shu-per.

## Q: What was a scribe?
A: Scribes were very important people in Ancient Egypt. They were taught to write and as many things in Egypt were written down they had very powerful jobs.

Training to be a scribe took a long time and was hard work. Boys started at special schools when they were six years old and continued until they were fourteen.

Scribes wrote on a type of paper called papyrus that was made of **reeds**. They wrote with brushes also made of reeds. Papyrus reeds grow beside the River Nile. They were cut into strips, placed side by side, pressed and then dried into paper sheets.

## Q: What did Egyptian writing look like?
A: Egyptian writing uses pictures as letters. Words are made up from the pictures put together. This writing is called **hieroglyphics**. You can see hieroglyphs on Pes-shu-per.

*These scribes are writing with reed pens on **scrolls** of papyrus paper. On the floor beside them are their inkwells and pen cases.*

17

## Q: Are these boats toys?

A: These boats are models. They were put in tombs so that the tomb owner had transport in the next life. Boats were very important to the Ancient Egyptians. There were many different types of boats used for different purposes. Some travelled short distances while others went far, taking **traders** and their goods to other countries.

## Q: Did everyone travel by boat?

A: The Egyptians nearly always travelled by boat and the River Nile was Egypt's greatest highway. Most people travelled in simple boats, but the Pharaoh and his family were carried in richly decorated boats. There were very few roads in Egypt. When travelling overland, most people walked. Some rich people could afford to be carried in special chairs by their servants. Sometimes traders brought their goods overland on the backs of donkeys.

*An Egyptian ship has just arrived at a foreign port.*

20

**Q: *Where did this painting come from?***
A: This picture is from the wall of a rich man's tomb. It shows him out fishing and hunting water birds. By placing it in his tomb, people thought that it would remind the dead man of the sports he enjoyed when he was alive.

**Q: *Did the Egyptians do a lot of fishing and hunting?***
A: The Egyptians liked to eat a lot of fish and water birds. Sometimes they would go out in boats and spear the fish or scoop them up in big nets. They caught the birds by throwing sticks at them. Sometimes they trained cats to bring back dead birds.

**Q: *How did they eat the fish and birds?***
A: Sometimes the fish were cleaned, cooked and eaten straight away. Or they were hung up to dry and then stored for eating later. The birds were plucked and cleaned and then roasted on spits.

*A fishing boat on the River Nile. The man in the middle of the boat is trying to kill geese with a stick.*

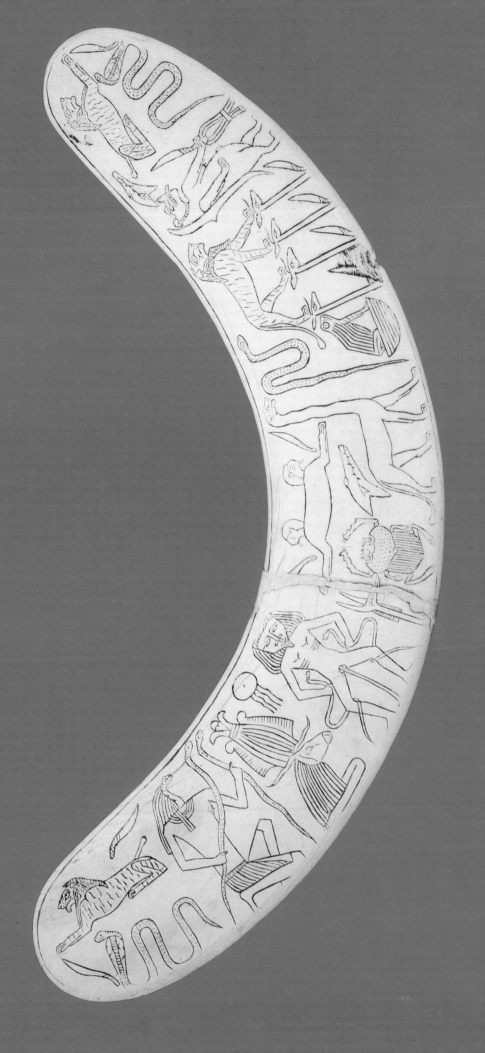

**Q: What is this?**

A: This is a magic wand. It is made of hippopotamus **ivory** and has pictures of different gods and goddesses carved on it. It was used to draw a circle around a person's bed. The Egyptians thought this would protect them from poisonous snakes and **scorpions**.

**Q: Were Egyptian doctors any good?**

A: Egyptian doctors were excellent **surgeons** and knew much about the human body.

**Q: Did only doctors treat ill people?**

A: The Egyptians believed that sometimes sickness was caused by the gods. The sick person was taken to a temple, where special priests worked as doctors.

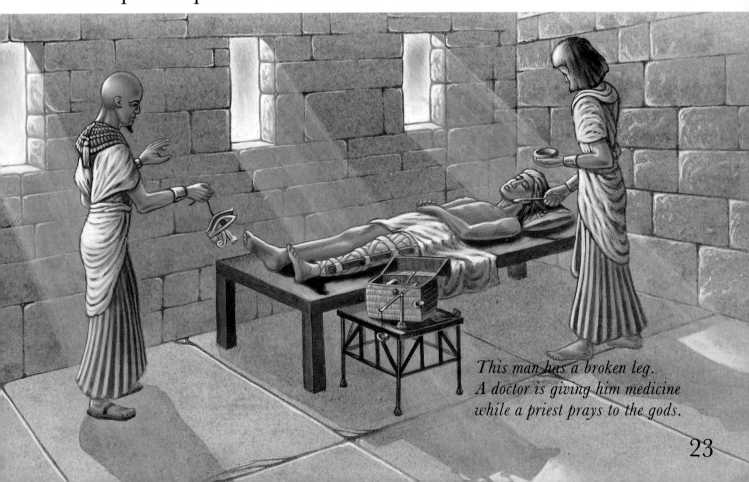

*This man has a broken leg. A doctor is giving him medicine while a priest prays to the gods.*

**Q: What is this jewellery made of?**
A: These bracelets are made of gold and decorated with coloured glass and **semi-precious** stones.

Egyptian men and women liked to wear lots of necklaces and earrings, rings and pendants.

**Q: What sort of clothes did they wear?**
A: The Egyptians wore long, flowing robes of fine linen. Noble women also sometimes wore dresses sewn with beads. Some pictures show Egyptian queens wearing dresses made from colourful feathers. If the weather was very cold some people wore woollen clothes to keep warm.

**Q: Did the Egyptians wear perfume or make-up?**
A: Egyptian men and women took great care in preparing their bodies before they dressed. They rubbed themselves with **perfumed oils** and painted their eyes with **kohl**.

*This noblewoman is being dressed for a special occasion. The maids bring her best jewels.*

25

26

**Q: *Where did this come from?***
A: This chair is from a rich Egyptian's house. It is made of expensive wood called ebony and covered in places with thin pieces of gold. Most chairs had short legs which were sometimes carved to look like animals' legs.

**Q: *Did everyone have chairs like this one?***
A: Most Egyptians had only a few pieces of furniture in their houses. Only rich people could afford wooden furniture. Usually chairs and tables were made of reeds.

**Q: *What was it like inside an Egyptian's house?***
A: Sometimes the floors of houses were covered with brightly-coloured tiles. Reed mats were then placed on top. Curtains made of reeds hung in the doorways. At night, the Egyptians lit clay lamps containing oil.

*This is an Egyptian house. One servant is grinding corn to make bread while another tends the plants. Sometimes, when it was very hot, people slept on the roof.*

28

**Q: Is this an Egyptian child's toy?**

A: Yes, it is called a paddle doll. It is made of wood that is painted. The hair is made of small beads of mud that rattle when the doll is shaken. It is 4,000 years old.

**Q: Did Egyptian children have many toys and games?**

A: Egyptian children played with spinning tops and had farm animals made of mud. They played with brightly-coloured leather balls. Another common game was tug-of-war.

**Q: How did their parents relax?**

A: Rich Egyptians liked to give large parties. They invited lots of people and there was always lots to eat and drink. Often, musicians, dancers, singers and acrobats entertained the guests.

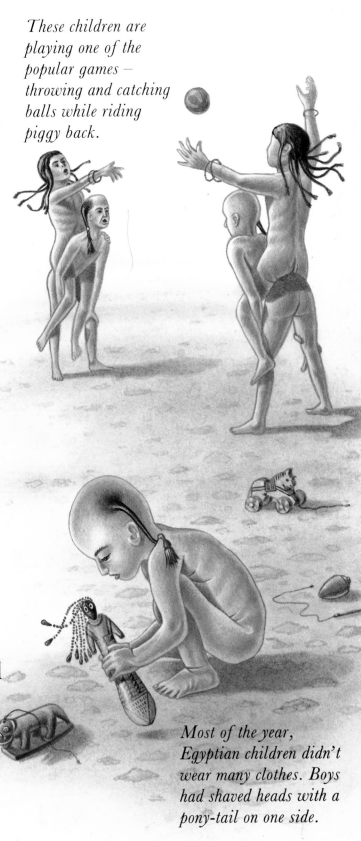

These children are playing one of the popular games – throwing and catching balls while riding piggy back.

Most of the year, Egyptian children didn't wear many clothes. Boys had shaved heads with a pony-tail on one side.

# GLOSSARY

**Bent Pyramid:** this pyramid was built for the Pharaoh Sneferu in about 2590 BC. The sides of the bottom half of the pyramid are steeper than the top half which makes it look bent. See page 13.

**departments:** a group of people who work together to make sure that everything in a certain area is running smoothly work in a department.

**Djoser:** Pharaoh of Egypt who reigned from about 2686-2667 BC.

**elaborate:** decorations on an object are described as elaborate when there are lots of them or they are very detailed.

**Giza:** a city in north-east Egypt on the west bank of the River Nile, opposite Cairo.

**Great Pyramid:** The largest stone building ever made. It is thought that this pyramid took 100,000 people twenty-three years to complete.

**hieroglyphics:** an early form of writing using pictures. First used in Egypt in about 3000 BC.

**intestines:** the name given to the insides of an animal (including humans) such as the stomach.

**ivory:** the hard white bone or tusk of the elephant, hippopotamus, walrus and narwhal. Ivory was often used for carving. This is no longer allowed as too many animals were being killed for their tusks.

**kohl:** a dark powder used by the Egyptians to decorate their eyes. Kohl is still used in make-up today.

**linen:** a lightweight material made from a plant called flax, usually white in colour. See page 23.

**minister:** someone who holds an office of state in a country. This means that they play an important part in the government of that country.

**natron:** the type of salt crystal used to dry the dead body during mummification.

**perfumed oils:** oils taken from plants and wood. These oils were rubbed on the body as perfume.

**preserved:** when something is preserved (like a fruit or a vegetable) it means that it is treated with chemicals that stop it from decaying (rotting) or slow down the decay.

**reeds:** tall grasses growing beside a river. In Egypt reeds grew next to the River Nile. They were used to make many things such as paper, pens, brushes, mats, curtains, chairs and tables.

**scorpions:** small animals with their skeletons on the outside of their bodies. They live in hot countries. They have a sting in their tail which is poisonous.

**scrolls:** scrolls are rolls of paper. The Egyptians used many scrolls of papyrus, which was their type of paper (see page 17). In Egyptian government and business everything was written down.

**semi-precious:** stones that are valuable but not as much as gemstones such as diamonds.

**Step Pyramid:** a pyramid designed for the Pharaoh **Djoser** by Imhotep (see page 15). It is the first pyramid and the earliest surviving stone building in the world.

**surgeons:** a doctor who performs surgical operations is called a surgeon. In surgery the body is cut open and the diseased part of the body taken out or treated.

**traders:** people who make their living by buying and selling goods.

# INDEX

A **bold** number shows the entry is illustrated on that page.
A word in **bold** can be found in the glossary.